Saints

Philip Sauvain

WAYLAND

LIFETIMES

Artists
Engineers
Saints
Writers

Series Editor: Alex Woolf
Editor: Liz Harman
Designer: Joyce Chester
Consultant: Norah Granger

Every attempt has been made to clear copyright for this edition. Should there be any inadvertent omission please apply to the publisher for rectification.

First published in 1997 by Wayland
@ Copyright 1997 Wayland Publishers Limited

Reprinted in 1999

This edition published in 2008 by Wayland
Wayland
338 Euston Road
London NW1 3BH

British Library Cataloguing in Publication Data
Sauvain, Philip Arthur
   Saints. - (Lifetimes)
   1. Saints - Biography - Juvenile literature
   I. Title
   270'.0922

ISBN 978 0 7502 5562 2

Typeset by Joyce Chester
Printed in China

Wayland is a division of Hachette Children's Books,
An Hachette Livre UK Company.
www.hachettelivre.co.uk

Contents

St Paul

St Paul was born about 2,000 years ago. At first his name was Saul. His parents were Jews, and Saul became a leader of the Jewish religion.
At that time Jews hated Christians, who lived in their land and believed that Jesus Christ was the son of God. Saul helped to persecute Christians, causing them to suffer for their beliefs.

◁ When he was travelling to a town called Damascus, Saul fell off his horse. While he was lying on the ground he saw a very bright light. A voice called out, *'Saul, Saul, why do you persecute me?'*

Saul could not see for three days after this.
He was sure he had heard Jesus speaking to
him. This is how Saul became a Christian. For
the rest of his life Saul tried to persuade people
in other lands to become Christians as well.
A person who does this is called a missionary.

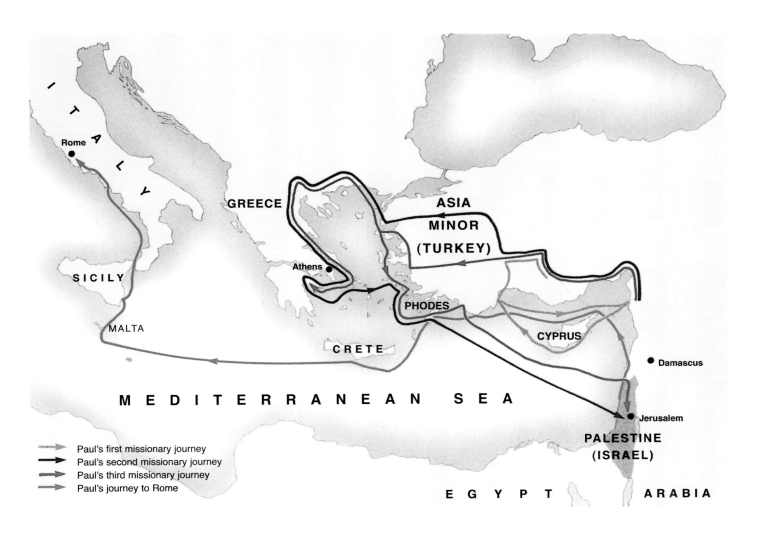

Paul's first missionary journey
Paul's second missionary journey
Paul's third missionary journey
Paul's journey to Rome

△ This map shows the places
St Paul went to as a missionary.

DATES	
AD10	Birth of St Paul
AD60	St Paul put in prison
AD67	Death of St Paul

Saul changed his name to Paul to show everyone he was now a changed man. Some people tried to stop him telling people about Jesus but he was not afraid and carried on with his work. Paul was hated by the Jews. They took him prisoner. Later he was sent to a city called Rome.

On the way his boat was shipwrecked on an island. ▷

◁ This stained glass window shows St Paul being brought in chains to Rome.

When Paul got to Rome, he was put in a prison below ground. When a cruel man called Nero became the ruler of Rome, Paul was executed. He was put to death for being a Christian.

A person who is killed because of their religion is called a martyr. Paul was a martyr, and this is why he was later made a saint. Many churches were named after him.

The most famous is in London. It is called St Paul's Cathedral. ▽

St Thomas Becket

Thomas Becket had a happy life as a boy.
People liked him. He wore fine clothes and loved
to hunt. When he was still a young man, the
English king, Henry II, made him Chancellor of
England. This was a very important job.

◁ Henry II (on the
left) with Thomas
Becket.

Thomas Becket and the king went riding together. They were good friends. Then, one day, everything changed. Henry decided to make Thomas Archbishop of Canterbury.
He was now in charge of all the churches in England even though he was not a priest.

Thomas Becket (on the left) with a priest. ▷

Thomas changed the way he lived. He ate bread and water instead of rich food and wine. At night he slept on a pillow made of stone. When he dressed, he put on a shirt made of prickly animal hair. In those days, church people thought that because Jesus Christ suffered pain, they should do so too.

The king was angry because his friend had changed. Later they had a bad quarrel. Henry was furious. *'Who will rid me of this troublesome priest?'* he said. Four knights standing near thought he meant what he said. On 29 December 1170, they rode to Canterbury. They burst into the cathedral with swords in their hands. *'Where is Thomas Becket, traitor to the king?'* they shouted. *'I am here, no traitor to the king, but a priest,'* he replied. At this the knights rushed forward. They killed Thomas with their swords.

◁ The murder of Thomas Becket.

DATES	
1118	Birth of St Thomas Becket
1162	St Thomas Becket becomes Archbishop
1170	Death of St Thomas Becket

The king was very shocked. Later he came to the place where Thomas had died. People had made it into a shrine. This means a very holy place.

△ Pilgrims on their way to Canterbury.

Thomas Becket was soon made a saint. People came from all over Britain and Europe to pray at his shrine. People who make a long journey like this are called pilgrims.

St Francis of Assisi

A boy called Francis Bernadone was born 800 years ago in a town called Assisi in Italy. He was the son of a cloth merchant.

◁ This is a painting of St Francis of Assisi.

Francis grew up a rich young man. He wore
fine clothes and was well liked by his friends.
He learned to be a knight.

One day he was taken prisoner by enemy
soldiers. After they let him go, he became ill.
He heard voices telling him to serve God.
This made him change his way of life.

Francis spent the
rest of his life
helping people who
were poor or sick.
He gave all his
money away.
He even quarrelled
with his father after
selling some of his
father's cloth to give
money to the poor.
He left home
wearing a ragged
cloak.

St Francis gives a
cloak away to a poor
man on the road. ▷

Francis asked other men to help him in his work. He called them friars, which means brothers. Francis wrote down what they had to do.

'They give everything to the poor. They are happy to have only one tunic patched inside and out,' he said. *'I want all the monks to work, not for money, but to show everyone it is better to work than be lazy.'*

A rich woman called Clare helped Francis to start a group, like the friars, for women. They were called the Poor Clares.

△ Clare, too, became a saint like Francis.

Francis spent much time alone by himself in the country. He loved birds and animals and talked to them as if they were people. He was later made the patron saint of animals.

◁ St Francis talks to the birds

After St Francis died a great church was built in Assisi. He was buried there and was soon made a saint.

This is the town of Assisi today. ▽

DATES	
1181	Birth of St Francis
1206	St Francis hears voices
1226	Death of St Francis

St Joan of Arc

Joan of Arc was born 600 years ago.
When she was thirteen years old, Joan saw a very bright light. At the same time she heard the voices of three saints. They said to her: *'Leave your village and go to help your king.'*

At that time Henry VI of England was also king of France. But the French wanted a prince called Charles to be their king.

DATES	
1412	Birth of St Joan
1425	St Joan hears voices
1431	Death of St Joan

◁ Joan of Arc.

With help from an army captain called Robert Joan was able to meet Charles. She told him about the saints who had talked to her. Charles believed her. He gave her a suit of armour and an army to lead. He told her to help the people in a French town called Orleans.

This town had been surrounded by English soldiers for many months. The people of Orleans were short of food.

When Joan came to Orleans, she gave everyone hope. ▷

Joan led the French soldiers into battle. Although she was wounded by an arrow, she drove the English away. She was only seventeen years old.

Joan won other battles as well. Her biggest success came when Charles was crowned King of France in July 1429.

Joan of Arc at the coronation of King Charles VII. ▷

But Joan had made many enemies. Some people thought a woman who dressed and fought like a man must be a witch. She was taken prisoner. The people who caught her sold her to the English.

◁ Joan is taken prisoner.

Joan was put on trial. Priests and judges tricked her into saying she was wrong and had not really heard the voices of saints. But later she said that she had heard voices after all. The judges said she must die.

Joan was tied to a wooden stake. She was borned alive still saying that God had told her to save France. 500 years later, Joan was made a saint.

△ Joan is tied to the stake in Rouen.

St Thomas More

Thomas More was born in England 500 years ago. Although he trained to be a lawyer, for a time, he lived as a monk. He wrote books. One book was about a perfect world. He called this world Utopia.

◁ Thomas More

DATES	
1477	Birth of St Thomas More
1529	St Thomas More made Lord Chancellor
1535	Death of St Thomas More

This was the Charterhouse in London where Thomas More lived as a monk. ▽

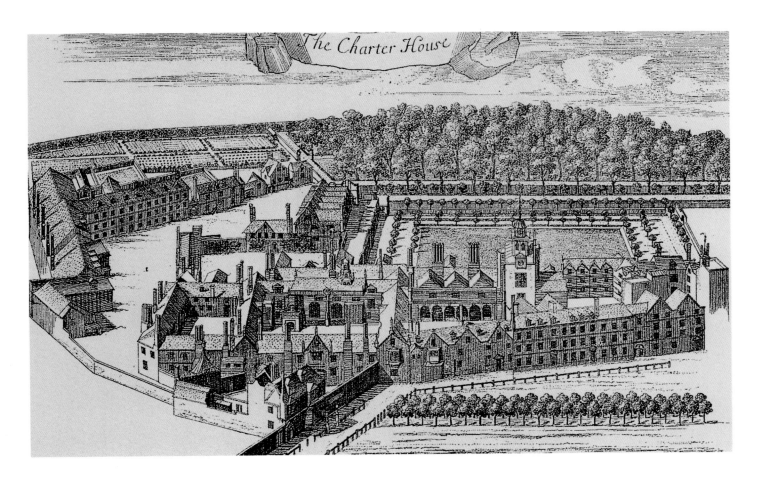

A famous writer wrote this about Thomas More. *'He is of medium height with pale skin. His hair is black with bits of yellow. His beard is thin and his eyes are grey. He always seems to have a smile on his face.'*

When Henry VIII became king, Thomas was given important jobs to do. Henry made him lord chancellor. This was the most important job in England. But Thomas did not want this job. He did not agree with the way the king was treating the Pope in Rome.

Henry and the Pope were quarrelling because Henry wanted to leave his wife and marry someone else. The Pope, who was head of the Roman Catholic Church, would not let him marry again. Henry was furious. He told people to obey him in future, not the Pope. Thomas More, like many other Roman Catholics, could not agree to this.

▽ The Tower of London in the time of Henry VIII.

The king sent Thomas More to prison in the Tower of London to make him change his mind. Thomas spent over a year there, but he would not give in. In the end the king had him put to death.

Thomas says goodbye to his daughter outside the Tower of London. ▽

A man with an axe cut off Thomas More's head. Thomas was very brave. He moved his beard away to stop it being cut by the axe. *'This has not offended the king,'* he said.

In 1935, 400 years after his death, Thomas More was made a saint.

St Bernadette of Lourdes

Bernadette was born in a small French town called Lourdes more than 150 years ago. As a child she was often ill. Living in a damp and dirty home only made her illness worse.

◁ Lourdes today.

Bernadette worked as a shepherd girl. In February 1858, aged 14, she went to look for firewood. When she saw her sister later on she had some news for her. She had seen a lady bathed in bright light in a cave called the Grotto of Massabielle.

The lady was *'a very young girl dressed in white'*, she said. *'About the same size as me,'* she added. Bernadette believed it was the Virgin Mary, the mother of Jesus Christ.

Bernadette sees the
Virgin Mary. ▷

News of what
Bernadette had seen
soon spread.
Thousands of people
went with her the next
time she went to the
cave. Once again,
Bernadette saw the
Virgin Mary, but no
one else did.

DATES	
1844	Birth of St Bernadette
1858	St Bernadette sees the Virgin Mary
1879	Death of St Bernadette

Bernadette said she had been told to dig up earth. When she did so, a spring of fresh water began to flow. People were amazed. They called it holy water. They thought it could heal people who were sick.

Bernadette was famous now. A visitor said *'she is a pretty girl with large eyes and very quiet.'*

St Bernadette. ▷

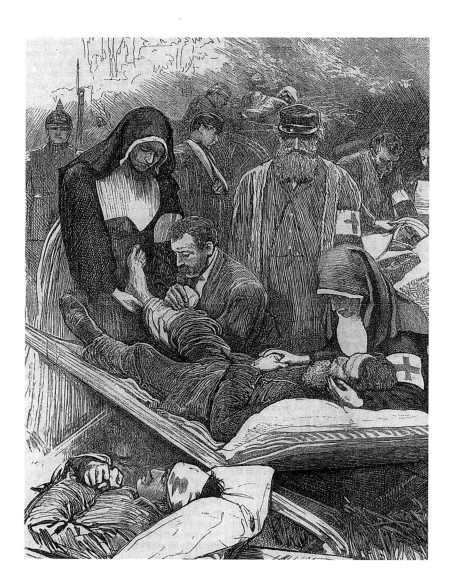

People who were crippled or ill came to Lourdes hoping to be cured. It soon became the most important place for pilgrims to visit in Europe.

◁ Bernadette worked as a nurse during a war in France in 1870. She helped wounded soldiers like those you can see here.

Bernadette found life hard now that she was famous. She became a nun but died in 1879 while she was still a young woman. Fifty years later she was made a saint.

Every year, millions of pilgrims visit the grotto where Bernadette saw the Virgin Mary, and bathe in the water from the spring.

Pilgrims wait to enter the Grotto of Massabielle. ▷

Timeline

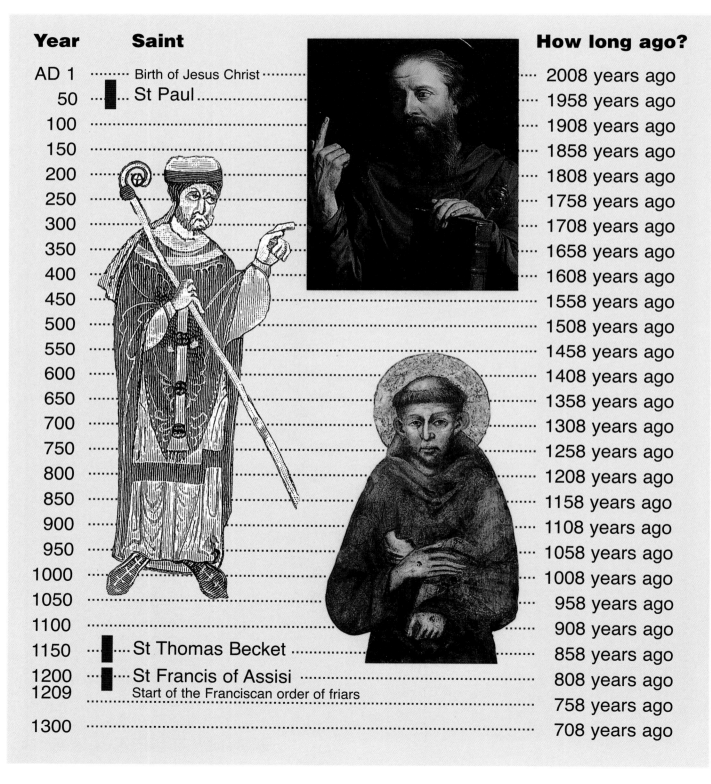

Year	Saint	How long ago?
AD 1	Birth of Jesus Christ	2008 years ago
50	St Paul	1958 years ago
100		1908 years ago
150		1858 years ago
200		1808 years ago
250		1758 years ago
300		1708 years ago
350		1658 years ago
400		1608 years ago
450		1558 years ago
500		1508 years ago
550		1458 years ago
600		1408 years ago
650		1358 years ago
700		1308 years ago
750		1258 years ago
800		1208 years ago
850		1158 years ago
900		1108 years ago
950		1058 years ago
1000		1008 years ago
1050		958 years ago
1100		908 years ago
1150	St Thomas Becket	858 years ago
1200	St Francis of Assisi	808 years ago
1209	Start of the Franciscan order of friars	
		758 years ago
1300		708 years ago

The grey bars in this timeline show the length of each saint's life, and the time when they lived.

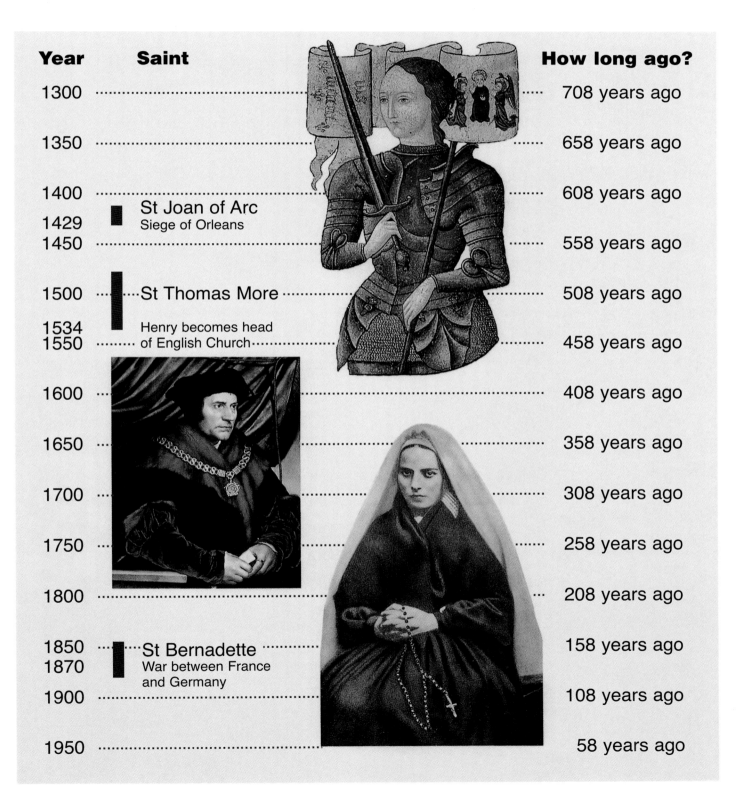

Year	Saint	How long ago?
1300		708 years ago
1350		658 years ago
1400		608 years ago
1429	St Joan of Arc — Siege of Orleans	
1450		558 years ago
1500	St Thomas More	508 years ago
1534	Henry becomes head of English Church	
1550		458 years ago
1600		408 years ago
1650		358 years ago
1700		308 years ago
1750		258 years ago
1800		208 years ago
1850	St Bernadette	158 years ago
1870	War between France and Germany	
1900		108 years ago
1950		58 years ago

Words to look up

abbey a building where monks or nuns live

Archbishop of Canterbury the head of the church in England

armour a suit of metal that soldiers used to wear for protection

cathedral a very large church

Christian a person who believes in Jesus Christ

execute to put someone to death

friar a man who lives like a monk but travels from place to place instead of living in an abbey

knight a soldier who wore armour and fought on horseback

martyr someone who is killed because of their religious beliefs

merchant someone who buys and sells goods, such as cloth

missionary someone who travels to other lands and tries to persuade people to change their religion

monk a man who spends much of his life in prayer

nun a woman who spends much of her life in prayer

persecute to ill-treat someone because of their religious beliefs

pilgrim a person who travels a long way to visit a shrine

Poor Clare a woman who lives like a nun and, following the example of St Clare and St Francis, gives everything she has to the poor

Pope head of the Roman Catholic Church

priest someone who serves God by being in charge of a church

religion what people believe in, such as being a Christian

shrine a holy place

spring a small stream which comes out of the ground

stake a thick pointed stick to which people were tied when they were burnt to death

traitor a person who is disloyal to their king or country

tunic a flowing garment reaching to the knees

vision something seen in a dream or in a blinding flash of light

Other books to look at

The Lives of the Saints by Nancy Martin, Wayland, 1986

Stories from the English Saints, St Pauls, 1994

Paul at Damascus by Penny Frank, Lion, 1989

St Francis of Assisi by Dorothy Smith, McCrimmon, 1987

St Joan of Arc by Brian Williams, Cherrytree, 1989

Saint Francis of Assissi by Joyce Denham and Elena Temporin, Lion Hudson PLc, 2007

Joan of Arc by Angela Bull, DK Publishing, 2000

Some places to see

St Paul's Cathedral in London – one of the biggest churches to be named after St Paul.

Canterbury Cathedral in Kent – where St Thomas Becket was murdered in 1170.

Assisi in Italy – where St Francis lived 800 years ago.

Orleans in France – where St Joan of Arc led French soldiers to victory in 1429.

Reims in France – where St Joan of Arc saw Charles VII crowned King of France.

Chinon in France – to see the statue of St Joan of Arc.

Rouen in France – where St Joan of Arc was burned at the stake in the market place in 1431.

The Tower of London – where St Thomas More was put to death in 1535.

Chelsea, London – to see the statue of St Thomas More in Cheyne Walk near the River Thames.

Lourdes in France – where St Bernadette saw a vision in 1858.

Index